WITH MY HANDS LIFTED UP

A Personal Study of Worship

DR. CATHERINE L. WHITE

With My Hands
Lifted Up

With My Hands Lifted Up
A Personal Study of Worship
Copyright © 2013
Author Dr. Catherine L. White
Email: info@anointedfire.com

Cover design: Anointed Fire™ Christian Publishing
Publisher: Anointed Fire™ Christian Publishing
Publisher's Website: www.afcpublish.com or
www.anointedfirepublishing.com

All scriptures noted in this book were taken from the King James bible unless otherwise noted.

ISBN-10: 0-9897560-8-4
ISBN-13: 978-0-9897560-8-2

Disclaimer: This book is designed to provide information and motivation to our readers. It is sold with the understanding that the publisher is not engaged to render any type of psychological, legal, or any other kind of professional advice. No warranties or guarantees are expressed or implied by the author, since every man has his own measure of faith. The individual author(s) shall not be liable for any physical, psychological, emotional, financial, or commercial damages, including; but not limited to, special, incidental, consequential or other damages. Our views and rights are the same: You are responsible for your own choices, actions, and results.

Introduction

Christian worship is the most beautiful and amazing thing I have ever experienced in life. I know that the only thing that will ever top it will be the experience that I will have around the throne. I love to worship God; it's like my life blood. There is so much to see, so much to hear and so much to feel in the presence of God. I love to watch other people of God worship as well. There are so many ways, styles and practices of worshiping GOD, and I always want to learn more. Not that I am trying out the newest fad, but I am always searching for deeper ways to express to the Savior how grateful I am for who He is to me and for what He continues to do in my life. One day, I decided I was going to look into this experience about raising hands in worship to the King of Kings, and I have never turned back.

Have you ever wondered why you hear ministers of God (ordinary people, worship leaders and Pastors) ask the congregation to lift their hands in worship? I often wondered about that myself, so I began to read the Word of God to see what it was about. I often wondered why people said, "Come on, people of God, lift those hands in the presence of your King." I decided to find out what happens when the people and the leaders who come to celebrate His name lift their hands in worship. Follow me on a quick journey through the Word of God and through the experiences of life as we discover what happens when we lift up our hands in worship.

Another thing we will deal with in this book is what is required of the worshiper. You must understand that you just can't come to God any old kind of way. We must come to Him in ways that please Him. We will spend some time learning how to approach GOD. After that, we will talk about what moving forward in worship looks like. Allow me to share with you what He has in His heart for me to share.

Table of Contents

Part I
What Happens With Lifted Hands

Chapter 1

Lifting up Holy Hands

As a child growing up in church, some things always kind of caught my attention; for example, when the people of God got "happy", and they would dance all around the church or cry. Some would "faint under the power of God." Some believers would run with no one chasing them. It was really an experience watching the people of God. I remember the first time my mother got "happy" in church. I remember telling myself I wouldn't sit with her anymore.

I also noticed that people would just raise their hands, which for me was strange because there was no apparent reason for that. I believed that I was a reasonable child, and their behavior just didn't make any sense to me. After all, no one had asked them a question. They did not seem to be trying to get anyone's attention. So what was this phenomenon? I just could not understand. When you are young, there are just some things you will better understand as time goes by, and I believed this was one of those things.

I left it alone until one day, as my relationship with God increased, I found myself almost without thought raising my hands just to tell Him thank you. There seemed to be such a connection with the Father when I lifted up my hands to thank Him and to just bless His wonderful name. I decided that I wanted to understand a little bit more about the lifting up of hands in worship, praise and adoration, so I began to dig.

When I first thought about the lifting up of hands in worship, my mind first went to Abraham and Isaac. I know that sounds kind of strange, but I could visualize the scene in Genesis 22. I could hear God making a demand on Abraham to worship Him at his best. I could also see Abraham as he took the knife in his hands in an act of obedient worship to God.

Genesis 22:9-12 reads, *"When they reached the place God had told him about, Abraham built an altar there and arranged the wood on it. He bound his son Isaac and laid him on the altar, on top of the wood. Then he reached out his hand and took the knife to slay his son. But the angel of the Lord called out to him from heaven, "Abraham! Abraham!"*
"Here I am," he replied.
"Do not lay a hand on the boy," he said. "Do not do anything to him. Now I know that you

fear God, because you have not withheld from me your son, your only son." (NIV)

I could see Abraham as he lifted up his hands to his God. God in heaven looked down on Abraham after seeing the depth of his devotion and finally said to him, *"Lay not thine hand upon the lad, neither do thou anything unto him: for now I know that thou fearest God, seeing thou hast not withheld thy son, thine only son from me" (Gen. 22:12).* It was this all or nothing worship to God that really got my attention. Abraham had made up in his mind that not even his child would separate him from true worship. I know it was a painful place for him, but he also knew that he was not alone. God had called him to this place, and it was at this place of sacrifice that Abraham grew even closer to his God. Abraham would not even let his own desires taint his worship. He would be clean before God, giving Him his all.

Worship requires a lot if we want to get it right. It requires obedience to the Word of God, will of God and way of God. We must have our minds made up that when we go to worship, we are going to give Him what He is requiring. God was very clear with Abraham about what He wanted. He said, "Take your son and offer him up as a sacrifice to me." Now, I know it bothers the people of God when we ask for a sacrificial offering, but this takes it to a whole different level. God is asking Abraham to give up his living dream. Isaac was Abraham's dream come true. He prayed for him, cried about him and waited for him. And now, here was God asking him to give up his dream as a sacrifice in worship? What would you do? What's a man to do when God asks for his all? We know the struggle because we have been there ourselves. God wants to take us to another place in worship, so He takes us to a place and asks us to give up our old places

and ways of doing things in order to receive the
new. That's a hard place for most of us,
because our sacred places are just that:
sacred. Oftentimes, we don't like the new place
because it's an unfamiliar place. It is a place of
total abandonment, total surrender and total
yes! The new place is a place of sacrifice.

Do you think Abraham wanted to let go
of what God had given him? No! He was living
in the place of an answered prayer. It is hard to
make sacrifices when you are in such a place.
We are comfortable with what we have, who
we have and where we are. We know this
place, and it's where we've been trying to get
to for a while. Now, God has the nerve to tell us
that it's time to move on. You need to give up
your place of comfort, so you advance further
in Him. Do it as an act of devotion. Do it as an
act of obedience. Do it as an act of worship.

Can you imagine holy hands lifted up in worship; hands lifted in sacrifice to God? Not perfect hands, but holy hands formed and shaped by obedience to the righteous God. What power there is in the presence of God; the power of sheer obedience.

I could see the trembling hands, but I also saw hands that are steady in their devotion to God. I can hear his heart as it says, "God, I'm going to do it your way even though it hurts. God, I'm going to do things your way, even if I cry straight through it. I am learning, Lord, that obedience is better than any sacrifice I offer. I'm also learning that obedience is a sacrifice in itself. My hands are not perfect, Lord, but I obey your call and direction." Open up your heart to see his hands. What do they look like in worship? We need obedient hands to lift up a sacrifice unto the Lord. But God not only wants obedient hands, He also needs clean hands.

1 Timothy 2:8 admonishes believers to *"lift up holy hands without wrath and doubting."* What strikes me as important is the specificity of the statement, "lift up holy hands." This tells me that my hands can be unholy, and if that's the case, I need not lift them up to the Lord. This statement makes me want to reconsider how, when and even what type of hands I am lifting to the Lord. I want my hands to be holy when I lift them up to Him. I want the hands that I lift up to Him to be cleansed of my own selfish will and ways. I don't want the sin of disobedience to cover my hands. I want truth and holiness to be reflected in my hands in worship. Psalm 24:3-4 asks a question, and it reads:

24:3: Who shall ascend into the hill of the LORD? Or who shall stand in his holy place?

24:4: He that hath clean hands, and a pure heart; who hath not lifted up his soul unto vanity, nor sworn deceitfully.

Who can stand in His holy hill? The answer is: He that hath clean hands and a pure heart. In order to stand on that holy hill; to stand in the place of worship, you will need hands that have been purged from the filthiness of the world. Leviticus tells us that the priests; the leaders of worship could not even so much as touch a dead body, or they would be defiled; their hands would be contaminated by death. Read Numbers 19:11-13:

19:11: He that toucheth the dead body of any man shall be unclean seven days.

19:12: He shall purify himself with it on the third day, and on the seventh day he shall be clean: but if he purify not himself the third day, then the seventh day he shall not be clean.

19:13: Whosoever toucheth the dead body of any man that is dead, and purifieth not himself, defileth the tabernacle of the LORD; and that soul shall be cut off from Israel: because the water of separation was not sprinkled upon him, he shall be unclean; his uncleanness is yet upon him.

We need clean hands to offer right sacrifices unto God.

As a child, I would feel uncomfortable when my hands were dirty, and I would not be okay until I washed my hands. In order for me to be able to do the next task or play the next game, my hands had to be clean. Also, we had a mother who, like most mothers, required that we wash our hands if we were going to sit down at the table. She did not want the dirt from the outside contaminating the food she was about to serve to us. We know that germs live in dirt. As in the natural, so in the spirit; the God that created heaven and earth does not want the sin of our lives to contaminate us in our worship. We have to be mindful of what we do with our hands, as we know they will be used in worship.

That word "clean" is the Hebrew word "naqiy" meaning: *innocent, free of blame, not guilty (Strong's #5355).* Those that lift their hands in worship to God must have clean hands. Whatever defiles our hands or our lives needs to be left alone; we shouldn't touch it. The Psalmist David says, *"The Lord rewarded me according to my righteousness: according to the cleanness of my hands hath he recompensed me, according to the cleanness of my hands in His eyesight" (Psalm. 18:20, 24).* Notice he said, "cleanness of hands in His eyesight." It is not cleanliness as we prescribe, but as He prescribes. We know exactly what we are doing with our hands, and we also know the things that displease Him. We also know what just straight-forward sin is. Avoid straight-forward sin if you can. That's like drowning your hands in mud before you go to worship God. We need clean hands that say, "I have worked on myself so what I do or am doing does not defile me or my relationship with the Lord. Not that I alone can fix me, but I have done my part to separate myself from those things that could or would defile or taint my walk with God."

If you'll recall in Isaiah 1, God spoke to Sodom and Gomorrah about the sacrifices they were making to Him. He basically said to them, "Just stop it! Everything you're bringing to me is not worth it, because your hands are filled with blood."

Isaiah 1: 10-15 says, *"Hear the word of the LORD, ye rulers of Sodom; give ear unto the law of our God, ye people of Gomorrah. To* *what purpose is the multitude of your sacrifices unto me? Saith the LORD: I am full of the burnt offerings of rams and the fat of fed beasts; and I delight not in the blood of bullocks, or of lambs, or of he goats. When ye come to appear before me, who hath required this at your hand, to tread my courts? Bring no more vain oblations; incense is an abomination unto me; the new moons and sabbaths, the calling of assemblies, I cannot away with; it is iniquity, even the solemn meeting. Your new moons and your appointed feasts my soul hateth: they are a trouble unto me; I am weary to bear them. **And when ye spread forth your hands, I will hide mine eyes from you: yea, when ye make many prayers, I will not hear: your hands are full of blood."***

The Lord was saying to them, bring no more empty worship, no more empty prayer or praise to Him. Even though many go through the ceremony, they have no real desire to change or be changed. You see, clean hands require the sacrifice of the heart, not just the ritual. Many can go through the motions of worship, but what is required is the heart being attached to the ritual. Real relationship produces real worship. Clean relationship with God produces clean fellowship and clean worship.

It's similar to engaging in sexual relations. If you have sex with someone you are not attached or attracted to, you will just go through the motions. There is no love lost because there is no love there. But, if it's someone you love, that would change the whole equation. Then you would be mindful of what you say or do in order to please the one that you are in love with. When you are with the one you love, many don't call that having sex; they refer to it as "making love". A person in love says in their hearts, "I want to be right for the person I love. I want to do it right for the person who loves me. I am looking to find a way to please the person who has my heart." So, a person in love searches out the heart of the person whom they love, to find out what pleases them, and they try to duplicate that. God told us not to bring Him anything that is not attached to our hearts. He doesn't like empty worship, and He would rather us not come to Him than to come to Him with an empty heart. You have to get your heart together before you approach Him. If you really love Him, you will try to do things that please Him. You would find out what He likes and do what pleases Him, and one thing He likes is clean hands.

Many will ask, "What are some of the things I need to leave alone? What are some dead things, old things that might defile my hands and my life; things that stop me from pleasing Him?" Some things are easier to ping than others. They are often the things or sins that we have already been delivered from. If you know that you are delivered from drugs, alcohol or sexual immorality, you know to stay away from these acts because they tamper with the cleanness of your hands and your walk with God. You have to stay away from the people, places and things that would draw you back into a lifestyle of sin. Of course we know this, but do we really do follow through with what we know? When we are weak, we often slide back into our comfort zones, comfort food and comfortable sins. We find ourselves like the dog returning to his vomit, or the sow to his wallowing. We find ourselves returning to those bad habits to soothe us; nevertheless, they don't soothe us, they just entrap us all over again.

Then there comes the tug of war between what we want to do for Him and what we want to do for ourselves. All too often, what we want for ourselves rises up as the winner, and the Savior is left on the outside looking in. The enemy then has a field day with us until spiritual reality sets in and we find that we need Jesus! Why can't we just separate ourselves from the defiled things and stay away from them for good? You have to fight to stay clean; fight to keep your lives, walk and conversations clean before the Lord! Sin always costs you. *"For the wages of sin is death but the gift of God is eternal life through Jesus . . ." (Romans 6:23).*

What is often harder to tag is the subtle stuff. It's those secret foxes that really spoil the vine; those things that are between you and you! Those secret sins aren't sins that we willingly bring before the Lord. They are our pet sins; the ones we don't want to give up or let God deal with. What do I mean? What about that lying, gossiping tongue; that mouth that both blesses God and curses our brother? That same mouth that we use to tell Him "thank you" is the same mouth we won't use to tell ourselves "no!" What about that deceitful heart that says, "I'm with you," but never joins the party? What about that act of doing a good deed for show and not out of love for the person or love for the Father? Secret sins are issues of our hearts, and it will take total surrender and spiritual surgery to remove that iniquity. But as we are submitted to Him in a loving relationship with Him, they will surface, and God will challenge us to deal with them. Truth be told, anything that will keep us from going forward in the things of God has the potential of defiling our relationship with Him.

One day, I found myself not able to pray like I ought to. I could not get the breakthrough in prayer that I was accustomed to. It seemed like there was a wall standing between me and my appointed destination: the presence of God. As I began to search my heart, the Lord revealed to me that there was some unforgiveness in my heart over something that a friend had done to me. I went before Him after that revelation and repented for having allowed unforgiveness to dwell in my heart. I forgave the person and released them to God. I told the Lord that I no longer held it against them. As I did this, I found the breaking in my own heart come forth. I was able to pray through and hear from Him; I was able to get direction from Him. I had hidden iniquity away in my heart so well that for a moment, I felt like I was praying past it. But if I regard iniquity in my heart, He will not hear me. *(See Psalm 66:18)*. It was hindering where I needed to go in God. It was defiling my hands, my conversation and my prayer life. I don't know anyone who is worth me losing my communion or communication with Him. He loved me enough to point it out so I could cleanse my hands before Him. Make a commitment to work on those hands so they will remain holy. When you work on them, you won't have to be ashamed when you lift them up in worship. You will be able to silence the accuser of the brethren.

Chapter 2

The Leader Intercedes

I'd like to turn my attention to what happens as the leader becomes the intercessor for the people of God. In order to do this, I would like to use King Solomon as my Old Testament case study.

King Solomon had it in his heart to build a house of worship for God. He received that as a legacy from his father, David. Scripture reminds us that the Lord told David he could not build Him a house of worship because he had shed too much blood. David was both a worshipper and a warrior. He knew what it took to fight in the spirit and in the natural. God told David that it was a noble idea for him to want to build a dwelling place for the Lord, but because of all the blood on his hands, he could not build it. Nevertheless, the son that He would give David (Solomon) would. According to the bible, David would later make preparation for the building of the Lord's house. David had the resources to do it and gave the project as an inheritance to his son. It was a part of the legacy that David left with Solomon.

Not long after the death of his father, Solomon went about the business of building the temple of the Lord. He made it according to the plans that his father had set forth. It was several years in the making. With no battles to fight and peace on every side, it was a joy and a pleasure to build the Lord's house. Solomon worked with a heart to please God, and God blessed the works of His hands. The project was completed, and the temple was magnificent; nevertheless, a place without a presence is worthless. You could build the finest cathedral; however, without the manifest presence of God; it would just be stone, brick and mortar, but no power. Solomon was excited about the completion of the temple, but he knew something was missing. Everything was in order, but he needed God. He needed God to show up and give His seal of approval. In the book of 2 Chronicles, both chapters six and seven talk about the dedication of the temple. This was a time of great celebration before our great God. This was the day that Solomon had been waiting for. He called the people of God together for the great celebration and dedication. Everything was in place. He was excited and the people around him were excited. The congregation had wonderment and excitement all at the same time. Can you imagine starting a project that

God laid in your lap and finally completing it?
Solomon went before the people to dedicate
the temple. The bible talks about the
preparations made for the dedication. Solomon
offered sacrifices of numbers that had not been
heard of. So great and massive was his
sacrifice that he had special altars built
specifically for this occasion. Solomon did not
want to impress people; he greatly sought after
the presence of God. He needed God to show
up; he earnestly entreated His presence. At the
dedication, as Solomon was before the people,
he postured himself in a way that invoked the
Spirit of the Lord. And the Word of the Lord
says:

2 Chronicles 6:12-14:

6:12: Then Solomon stood before the altar of
the Lord in front of the whole assembly of
Israel and spread out his hands.

6:13: Now he had made a bronze platform, five
cubits long, five cubits wide and three cubits

high, and had placed it in the center of the outer court. He stood on the platform and then knelt down before the whole assembly of Israel and spread out his hands toward heaven. **6:14:** He said: "Lord, the God of Israel, there is no God like you in heaven or on earth-you who keep your covenant of love with your servants who continue wholeheartedly in your way."

Solomon took this time before the presence of the Lord and in the face of this whole congregation to thank God for being faithful to them. He humbled himself before his God and in front of His people. Although he was king, he humbled himself and became a servant in the form of a priest. He made intercession for himself and for the people. He reminded and thanked God for being a God who keeps covenant. He told God and His people that He had been merciful to them, and specifically to him, as he walked before Him with all his heart. He is God in heaven and earth, and there is no god like Him anywhere. The bible says he spread forth his hands before heaven in the form of petitioning God to hear him as he prayed.

"Then Solomon stood before the altar of the Lord in front of the whole assembly of Israel and spread out his hands. Now he had made a bronze platform, five cubits long, five cubits wide and three cubits high, and had placed it in the center of the outer court. He stood on the platform and then knelt down before the whole assembly of Israel and spread out his hands toward heaven" (2 Chronicles 6:12-13 NIV). As you read further into 2 Chronicles 6, you will discover that Solomon made the prayer of dedication and he interceded for Israel. What happened next? 2 Chronicles 7:1-3 tells us that the glory of God came in.

2 Chronicles 7:1-3:

7:1: Now when Solomon had made an end of

praying, the fire came down from heaven, and consumed the burnt offering and the sacrifices; and the glory of the LORD filled the house. **7:2:** And the priests could not enter into the house of the LORD, because the glory of the LORD had filled the LORD'S house. **7:3:** And when all the children of Israel saw how the fire came down, and the glory of the LORD upon the house, they bowed themselves with their faces to the ground upon the pavement, and worshipped, and praised the LORD, saying, For he is good; for his mercy endureth for ever.

As the man of God stretched forth his hands before the Lord in prayer and intercession, the power of God fell; fire came down from heaven and consumed the offerings that were laid before the Lord. The glory of the Lord filled the temple of the Lord. The priests could not enter in because His presence so filled the place that there was no room for the flesh of man. How awesome is that?! When the leaders of God's people pray with uplifted hands for the people of God, things happen in heaven, and the power of God is unleashed to deal with the flesh of man. When intercession is made for the people, God gets involved and the consuming fire of God is released.

I don't know about you, but I want my leaders calling out my name in prayer and intercession. I want my leaders to talk to God about my crazy, mixed up ways. I want them to have a little talk with Jesus and tell Him all about my troubles. I need my leaders covering me and asking God to deal with me as they pray!

As the leaders lay before the Lord, they surrender and cast their burdens upon Him, for He careth for them. They give us over to the only One who can handle who we are and what we are going through. They ask for His kingdom to come and His will to be done here in the earth for our lives. Solomon released God to deal with His people as he made prayer and intercession before them. As Solomon prayed, God began to answer. It is always good for us to allow our leaders time before the Lord, so they can intercede for us. After all, they watch for our souls according to Hebrews13:17. Give them the time and space where they can comfortably cry out to God for us so that the fire of God that we need will be released in our lives. We need the fire of God released in our lives to burn up old habits, bad thoughts and wicked ways. We need the fire of God to purify our minds, cleanse our hearts and purge our sins from us. We need the fire of God! Know of a surety that when the leaders speak, God listens and moves.

So much has been broken up in and over my life as I asked my leaders to intercede and cry out to God on my behalf. Deliverance, healing and direction is released as I trust them to carry me before the Lord. That does not negate my own need for personal intercession, but it gives me an added bonus as two are touching and agreeing on things in this earth *(See Matthew 18:19).*

As a leader who watches over the souls God has given into my hands, I am commanded to praise Him and to go into the sanctuary and lift my hands to bless Him. When I lift up my hands in the presence of The Lord, I am following what the Word of God says in Psalm 134: 1-2:

134:1: Praise the Lord, all you servants of the Lord who minister by night in the house of the Lord.

134:2: Lift up your hands in the sanctuary and

praise the Lord.

I am commanded to go into the place where the people of God worship and be the first partaker of worship. I am commanded not just to go, but to do something. As leaders, it is not enough for the people to worship, but they must see their leaders in worship. We are their examples. We show them the way into the holy of holies. We point them in the direction of the secret place of the Most High. We are the ushers into the sanctuary of praise. The people of God look to us to show them how to "get there."

Sometimes, we want to wait in our offices until the sanctuary is HOT, but we ought to be there when the fire starts, or we at least should be one of the fire starters! As the people see us go up, they will go up. As they see us worship, they will worship. As they see us be still and know that He is God, they learn how to rest in His presence. As leaders, we show them the ways of righteousness and holiness in the sanctuary of God. How will they hear without a preacher or teacher? This is for the leaders: Don't forget to lead.

Chapter 3

Hands Raised In the Battle

You know, we as believers are some of the most "sometiming" people. I know that's not proper English, but bear with me for a moment. Sometimes we go through the fires of a storm. Sometimes we go up, and sometimes we go down. Your true worship is not tested in the times when everything is going well; it's when all hell breaks loose and the battles rage in your life that worship is tested. Will you lift your hands to Him in worship when you really want to cry? Will you bless the Lord at all times with praises in your mouth?

People of God, I know that sometimes we do go through challenges. More often than not, we are faced with hard times and problems that seem to want to pull us away from our place of worship. We want to press into His presence, but the warfare is so hot and heavy that we retreat back to our comfort zones. In Exodus 17:8-13, the Bible talks about a time when the people of God were faced with a battle. The Bible says, *"Then came Amalek and fought with Israel in Rephidim. And Moses said unto Joshua, 'Choose us out men, and go out, fight with Amelek: tomorrow I will stand on the top of the hill with the rod of God in mine hand.' So Joshua did as Moses had said to him, and fought with Amalek: and Moses, Aaron and Hur went up to the top of the hill. And it came to pass when Moses held up his hand, that Israel prevailed: and when he let down his hand, Amelek prevailed."* You see people of God, Moses stood with his hands raised on the hill before the people of God as they battled with their enemy Amelek. As we read above as long as his hands were raised the children of Israel would be winning the battle. But as soon as Moses hands went down their enemy began to defeat them. Scripture says, *"But Moses hands were heavy . . ."* Moses's hands came down he was weary from the pressure of lifting them. When he was younger, it probably would have been easier to do, but now that he was older, it was a bit more difficult.

Sometimes, we get weary in the battle of pressing in. It becomes difficult pressing through the principalities and powers to obtain what we need from God. On my trip to Ghana, I discovered that when I lifted up my hands to worship the Lord, it was much easier to witness breakthrough. The atmosphere was not as layered with heavy demonic activity as there is here in America. This made my worship experience seem much freer. Here in America,

I have sometimes found it difficult to get into an atmosphere of praise. Sometimes, the struggle is so difficult that it causes us moments and seasons of great frustration. As believers, we often get downhearted and depressed. In frustration, we ask the Lord for help, and help He does.

The text goes on to say, *"And they took a stone, and put it under him, and he sat thereon; and Aaron and Hur stayed up his hands, the one on one side and the other on the other said; and his hands were steady until the going down of the sun" (Exodus. 17:12).* Aaron and Hur noticed that there was a problem and Moses needed help. They came to the aid of the man of God. They sat him on a rock and held up his hands. I want to encourage you man of God, woman of God and child of God. In your frustration of pressing into worship, God will see your struggle, and

He will assign angels to come alongside you to assist you. He will set you on a ROCK! Then, He will send a servant of the Lord to pray with you or worship with you until breakthrough comes. While your hands begin to weaken in the battle for pure worship, at times you will feel supernatural strength to go the extra mile. That supernatural strength comes from heavenly Aarons and Hurs. They were sent by the Father to strengthen you much like He did for His Son, Jesus, in the garden of Gethsemane.

Trust me; you are not alone in your pressing. God wants you to receive your desired effect. He wants to commune with you; He wants you to fellowship with Him. Your hands lifted up in worship invites the presence of God into your struggles and traumas. It gives God the green light to go in and exact punishment upon your enemies. It gives Him the permission to do what He wants to do: save, heal and deliver you. Uplifted hands say to God, "This may be greater than me, but it is not greater than YOU!" It causes Him to stand up in your circumstances and show Himself as your God. There is great power in raised hands in your place of challenge and your place of pain.

Lifting your hands to worship God in your struggle is difficult, not only because the battle is long and wearisome, but also because of the type of enemy we face. He does not play fair. He sends spirits to attack us when we press into the presence of God. The enemy systematically works against the worshipper. He tells us that we are too tired to endure the struggle. He sends discouragement and the spirits of oppression and depression to slow our roll, weigh us down and burden us until we feel breakthrough in this area is impossible.

But the devil is a liar! No weapon formed against us will prosper. We will break through in the areas of worship until victory is ours.

We must use the resources God sends to us to thwart the enemy. We need to use our prayer partners to help us worship and praise our way through. Allow the angels of God to minister to us as we feel overwhelmed.

Also, take into consideration that the battle for our souls is as the Savior lifted up on the tree. You want to talk about hands lifted up in battle, hands lifted up in intercession; we need to see the Savior. Crucifixion required your hands and legs to be tied to a tree after being scourged. It called for a long and painful death. Jesus was not an ordinary man. As a matter a fact, Pilate found no cause to put Him to death (*See Luke: 23*). But because of the people, Pilate consented to have Him crucified.

Because He was hated by the Jews, Jesus received more punishment than the average person. He was beaten beyond recognition. Isaiah 52:14 says His visage (face) was marred more than any man. The bible also says He had no beauty that we should desire Him. (*See Isaiah 53:2*). As we read further in Isaiah, it states: *"Who hath believed our report? To whom is the arm of the LORD revealed? For he shall grow up before him as a tender plant, and as a root out of a dry ground: he hath neither form nor comeliness; and when we shall see him, there is no beauty that we should desire him. He is despised and rejected of men; a man of sorrows, and acquainted with grief: and we hid as it were our faces from him; he was despised, and we esteemed him not. Surely he hath borne our griefs, and carried our sorrows: yet we did esteem him stricken, smitten of God, and afflicted. 5 But he was wounded for our transgressions, he was bruised for our iniquities: the chastisement of our peace was upon him; and with his stripes we are healed."*

The Savior endured pain, sorrow and suffering. His hands were not tied to the cross; they were nailed to it for you and me. On the cross, He was interceding for our souls. He took our place on that cross. His hands were stretched wide toward God. The enemy was having a field day because he thought he'd won. But thank God for Resurrection Sunday! The Savior got up from the grave for you and me. He waged war with the enemy of our souls, for our souls, and won! His hands were raised in the battle by the enemy himself, but Christ took victory and handed it to us. Glory to God in the highest! That's why we must understand that the Greater One is with us. He is fighting for us and interceding on our behalf on a daily basis. He ever liveth to make intercession for us, according to Hebrews 7:25.

People of God, know that there is a constant war going on daily for the souls of men. The enemy is fighting a losing battle, but we should not cooperate with him and help him win. We cannot risk allowing our hands to go down in the battle of interceding for our loved ones. We cannot let our tired bodies or wearied hearts give place to the enemy. We must press on; press in until we get what we have petitioned the Father for, even as our Savior did. Souls are at stake. Whose report will you believe? We shall believe the report of the Lord. His report says VICTORY!

Chapter 4

What It Means For Me

When I lift my hands in worship, I am surrendering everything I am to Him. I turn over my challenges, my issues, my mistakes, my worries and everything else to the One who is more than able. I lift my hands in order to take my hands off of those things. I lift my hands to Him saying, "Here it is, Lord, and here I am."

Now sometimes, it is hard to lift my hands. Sometimes, there are things that I think "I" can handle. (I'm sure you can relate). And try as I might, I find myself putting myself in the middle of a mess. Then I have to come back with lifted hands in complete surrender to the "one who is able to keep me from stumbling…"

You see, when I lift my hands, I am saying to the Lord, "I need You, and I trust You to work it out for my good." I'm saying to Him, "I give up. I'm tired of trying to work this thing out on my own. I've tried over and over again, and I just cannot make this thing work. I failed at this one. Please help me, Lord, because I cannot help myself."

People of God, I need His presence in my life. I long for Him; I press forward to experience true and pure worship. You see, true worship is a communication of the heart of man to the true and living God. It is a reaching out and up to Him.

Also, when I lift my hands to Him, I am connecting my heart to His heart. It's like a reconnection of that umbilical cord; it's that connection that gives life-changing blood. I am reaching up to Him, and He is reaching back to me. I am connected to my Source of life and His life-giving blood. It is at this time that I can feel the stream of Calvary's blood flowing over everything, every sin that may be covering me. His blood is powerful enough to wash it all away! I feel closer to Him, and I sense the heartbeat of His love over me and in me.

It's also like that little child who wants their parent to pick them up. Oftentimes, in those instances, we teach our children to verbalize what they want, so they understand and we understand what they want. During a struggle, I am saying the same thing to my heavenly Father. "Father, I want You to take me up; I want to go up. I want to go far beyond my circumstances and into Your arms of love and compassion. I want to go up and away from where I am to that secret place of the Most High." I am saying, "Lord, I want You to hide me in Your pavilion. Oh God, carry me on the wings of eagles into that secret place. Take me up, Lord, where I can get healed, cleansed, renewed and restored."

When I lift my hands in worship, I lose all track of time; I lose myself in the presence of God; I free myself from the things that have bound me, because now I am in the safety zone with my Daddy! That's where my help is: in His presence. My strength is in His presence; my hope is in His presence, and so is my peace. The wonderful thing is God wants me and He wants you there: in His presence. He is always bidding us to come up, to come away with Him. The Father loves to take us up and into His presence to show us who He really is. He wants to lavish His love upon us.

As the Song of Solomon says, "I want to go up. I need to go up. Take me up, Father!"

When I lift my hands, I yield myself to whatever He desires to do and wherever He wants to take me. When I was young in the faith, I would lift my hands trying to copy what I saw others do. But now that I have lived a little bit more, when I do raise my hands to Him in worship, I do it with a better understanding. I want to be close to Him; I want to be with Him. Glory to God, all of me longs to be with all of Him!

I am at the point in my life that I can be in the supermarket, feel His presence, and lift my hands to Him in worship. I can be sitting in my car, and the Holy Ghost will slip in there. Right then and there, my car becomes the tabernacle of the Lord. My hands being raised before the Lord invites Him to come and have

His way in me! Don't you want Him to have His way with you?

Some people feel that experiencing His presence is only for Sunday morning, and anything outside of that is excess, but I submit to you that I want all the excess that I can receive. I want His presence every day of my life. I want to feel Him in my car, my room at work and riding with me as I commute to work. I want to know that He is with me, even if I walk through dark places according to His Word (*See Psalm 23*). At my job, I will lift my hands; on the subway, I will lift my hands. In my room, I will raise my hands in worship to invite Him to be with me. It is an invitation to intimacy.

Part II

What Worship Requires Of You

Chapter 5

Relationship

If we want to experience a move of God, we must first work on our relationships. We want the will of God produced, but in order to do His will, we must know His will. In order to know His will, we must know Him. In order to know Him, we must have a relationship with Him.

Relationship is defined as:
1. A connection, association, or involvement.
2. Connection between persons by blood or marriage.
3. An emotional or other connection between people: the relationship between teachers and students.

4. A sexual involvement; affair.

Reference: Dictionary.Reference.com

Understand that the King of Kings and the Lord of Lords is looking to connect with you. He's looking to be involved in your life. He's also looking for you to be involved with the work that He is trying to produce on this earth; however, He's not looking for just anyone. He's looking for those who will surrender all in order to be connected to Him. We all know relationships are funny and very tricky. Most of all, relationships take work. Oftentimes, we don't mind working on things that bring about an instantaneous result; nevertheless, we don't seem to want to give that same drive to the things that require time. He is calling for those who are willing to risk and give all to share in the work of the Kingdom. Willing workers are the type of people He wants to be in a relationship with. He is looking for Kingdom-minded folk. The Lord is not looking for those

who just want to build up their happy church
and go on their happy way. No. He is looking
for those who will sell all and be a part of this
end-time work. Those who will say, "Whatever
the cost may be, I'll do it in order to please the
One who called me into the Kingdom for such
a time as this."

He is seeking a love relationship, not
just a work relationship. He wants a love affair
that will last for all time; one that is not defined
by time or space, but just a totally unhindered
submission to His will, His Word and His way.
He's not looking for bargainers who say, "Lord
if you save me from this situation, I will do Your
will." Such a mindset serves as a barrier
between ourselves and the Savior. If He never
does another thing in my life, He's already
done enough! The Father is seeking the kind of
relationships that says, "I'm satisfied with you,
Lord. You are the One I've been seeking, and

You have been seeking me. This kind of relationship is never one-sided. Take note of what Peter said to Jesus in Luke 18:28. *"Then Peter said, Lo, we have left all, and followed thee. And he said unto them, Verily I say unto you, There is no man that hath left house, or parents, or brethren, or wife, or children, for the kingdom of God's sake, Who shall not receive manifold more in this present time, and in the world to come life everlasting."*

Whatever you give up for the cause of Christ, the work of the ministry and for the Kingdom of God, He will return to you more in this life and in the life to come: everlasting life. You don't lose when you release to God; He will return it to you and love on you because of it. You win on both sides when you are in a relationship with the Lord! You will not be able to beat God giving. John 3:16 says that God gave His very best for us: His only Son! The bible says in Romans 5:7-8, *"Scarcely for a righteous man will one die: yet peradventure for a good man would some even dare to die. But God commended His love toward us in that while we were yet sinners Christ died for us."* He wanted a relationship with us, and He loved us so much that while we were still in our sins, He prepared the way for us. He keeps giving every day. Anyone in a relationship with you wants to demonstrate how they feel about you. God demonstrated His love for us, and He demonstrates it day and night. But we must be in the place where we want and need to give Him more of ourselves. The King requires more; the King deserves more.

Being in relationship with the King of Kings is a win-win situation for us. As we give ourselves more in relationship with Him, He pours more of Himself into us. When people see us, they will see the Father within us. I want to be so in tune with the Lord that folks will say that I talk just like my Father. Jesus was so united with the Father that He could rightfully say, *"He that hath seen me hath seen the Father" (John 14:9).* I want to be so into Him that my testimony would be like the testimony of Christ. The relationship between the Father and the Son is just that air-tight! When you saw One, you absolutely saw the Other; even if you didn't believe. Jesus said that He only did those things that please the Father. He said that He came to do the Father's will. That's how a relationship works: We should do what pleases Him and what He wants us to do.

Coupled with working on our relationship with the Lord, we must also work to improve our relationships with the people of God. Jesus had favor with both God and men. In order for Kingdom work to go forward, we must work with the people in the Kingdom. Servitude, humility, faithfulness and trustworthiness will get you far in working with the people of God.

In John 13, Jesus gave us the most perfect example of servanthood and humility: John13:3-17 reads, *"Jesus knowing that the Father had given all things into his hands, and that he was come from God, and went to God; He riseth from supper, and laid aside his garments; and took a towel, and girded himself. After that he poureth water into a basin, and began to wash the disciples' feet, and to wipe them with the towel wherewith he was girded. Then cometh he to Simon Peter: and Peter saith unto him, Lord, dost thou wash my feet? Jesus answered and said unto him, What I do thou knowest not now; but thou shalt know hereafter. Peter saith unto him, Thou shalt never wash my feet. Jesus answered him, If I wash thee not; thou hast no part with me. Simon Peter saith unto him, Lord, not my feet only, but also my hands and my head. Jesus saith to him, He that is washed needeth not save to wash his feet, but is clean every whit: and ye are clean, but not all. For he knew who should betray him; therefore said he, Ye are not all clean. So after he had washed their feet, and had taken his garments, and was set down again, he said unto them, Know ye what I have done to you? Ye call me Master and Lord: and ye say well; for so I am. If I then, your Lord and Master, have washed your feet; ye also ought to wash one another's feet. For I have given you an example, that ye should do as I have done to you. Verily, verily, I say unto you, The servant is not greater than his lord; neither he that is sent greater than he that sent him. If ye know these things, happy are ye if ye do them."*

If Jesus; the Lord of glory, served His disciples in humility; shouldn't we serve even the more, being children of God? He left us an example. He said if we do the same, we will be happy. Shouldn't we be doing whatever we can to further the Kingdom? Shouldn't we lay aside every weight so that we can work with the people of God that He has called us to work with?

Sometimes we make it harder for ourselves, because we desire to be served rather than serve. Jesus says the leader should be the first servant. What must I do so the program of God can go forward? Who do I need to connect with, be in relationship with, and partner with so the plan of God can progress forward? Be willing to roll up your sleeves and put your hands to the plow. You are not too good, too anointed nor too gifted to use those gifts to work on the floor or in the kitchen. As you are the example before the people, they will follow your lead. As people of God see the leader serve, connect and be in relationship with others; they will find it much easier to follow the leader.

Jesus came to serve and give His life as a ransom for many. He came serving the people of God that rejected Him. The Bible says in John 1 that He came to His own, and His own did not receive Him. Their rejection did not cause Him to stop serving them. In spite of all the challenges He faced, He continued serving because the will of the Father was greater than the rejection of men. People will not always want to work with you, but you must persevere because of the Kingdom. Know that you are doing a good work, and you can't stop!

It is also necessary for you to be in place when you are supposed to be there.

Faithfulness is critical for accomplishing any work in the Kingdom. We don't always feel like being where we need to be, but we must remain faithful to get the task done. Can God and the people of God trust you to be faithful? Can we know that when the assignment is given to you, we don't have to worry about it? Are you really the one, or should we look for another?

But many say they don't want to work with this sister or that brother, even though the one they don't want to work with is the one their Pastors told them to work with. People of God, trust your Pastor. He or she knows who is skilled in one area, who needs work in other areas, and how to kill two birds with one stone. Some people of God have the ability to pull some things out of you or place some things in you. As you surrender yourself to the relationships that God has ordained, He works on you and the other person. Sometimes it is subtle; other times it is very obvious. In the beginning, it may be hard and rocky, but if you are in place working, being worked on and being faithful, the leader will be able to see you and trust you with more. *"His lord said unto him, Well done, good and faithful servant; you have been faithful over a few things, I will make you ruler over many things: enter into the joy of your lord" (Matthew 25:23).*

In addition, relationship (by definition) has to do with connections by blood. How many of you know that we have been purchased by God with the precious blood of the Lamb? The Lamb of God who takes away the sin of the world is the One that we ought to be in relationship with. He died that we may have life! We live for Him because He died, rose from the dead, and lives for us and with us. That's why we ought to give the Lord praise. His blood covers and keeps us. His blood heals our wounded hearts, souls and bodies! We must thank Him every day for His blood!

Chapter 6

An Invitation to Intimacy

We know the scene: the officer pulls the criminal over, tells them to basically assume the position, and that person is now exposed to whatever the officer would do. It's pretty scary to think about. Thank God for trustworthy officers who handle their positions with integrity and in a professional manner. But understand this: Guilty or not, the person is exposed.

We don't like to be exposed. The only time we want to be exposed is during times of our own choosing. During times of intimacy, we don't mind raising our hands, reaching up or reaching out. We don't mind getting lost where we are, and with whomever we are with. Understand that raising our hands makes us both exposed and vulnerable. Let us dive in a little bit on both of those concepts as they relate to intimacy.

First of all, let's deal with the feeling of being exposed. Think about the physical position that we are in when we worship the Lord. Our hands are lifted, and more than likely, our eyes are closed. In addition, we are either alone with the Lord or in a group of people basking in His presence. In worship, we are focused on the One who loves us, died for us and gave His life for us. We are not looking to protect ourselves in this environment. We are only looking to Him! We are literally exposed. Does anyone really like the feeling of being exposed? The word "expose" means to "put somebody in an unprotected situation: make somebody experience something: allow something to be seen." *(Reference: Microsoft Encarta College Dictionary).* When we lift up our hands in worship, we expose ourselves to Him. We put ourselves in a position where the only One who can cover and protect us against the stares of others, the wars of the enemy or the challenges in our life is the Lord. We expose our hearts to Him as we raise our hands.

When I worship Him, I see myself as I lift my hands in His presence, uncovering or exposing all that I am to Him. I am not hiding any of my frailties or faults. I am allowing the light of His love to expose the film on my heart! He can't miss a thing anyway, but I am putting myself in the position for Him to read the motives and the intent of my heart. I am allowing myself to be seen by Him. Psalm 139:23-24 says, *"Search me, O God, and know my heart: try me, and know my thoughts: And see if there be any wicked way in me, and lead me in the way everlasting."*

What David is doing here is exposing himself to God. He is basically saying, "Lord, look inside of me; let the light of Your love search me. I am not covering who I am but laying my heart bare before You. Search and know me, oh God; not just my heart, but also try, examine and scrutinize who I am as a personal worshipper. Father, look in my mind and know, discriminate, distinguish and be acquainted with my thoughts; make sure that there is no wickedness in me." The position of raised hands causes everything that is in you to be revealed.

Hebrews 4:13
"Neither is there any creature that is not manifest in his sight: but all things are naked and opened unto the eyes of him with whom

we have to do."

As we raise our hands before Him in worship, we are naked and open before Him. We are truly exposed to Him, but He will not harm us; He will only heal us as we are in that position before Him. His love is our covering and protection from the wiles of the devil. Praise His mighty Name, His presence envelops us so that we are naked and not ashamed!

The next word we will review in relation to intimacy is the word "vulnerable." The word vulnerable, according to dictionary.com, means:
1. capable of or susceptible to being wounded or hurt, as by a weapon: a vulnerable part of the body.
2. open to moral attack, criticism, temptation,

etc.: an argument vulnerable to refutation; He is vulnerable to bribery.

3. (of a place) open to assault; difficult to defend: a vulnerable bridge.

4. Bridge. having won one of the games of a rubber.

With our hands raised, as the definition states, we are "capable of or susceptible to being wounded or hurt as by a weapon." The wonderful thing about our Lord is that He comes not to hurt but to take the hurt away. Though we may be in a vulnerable position, we are sheltered by His everlasting arms; we are covered under the shadow of His wings! His arms of love keep us in the center of fellowship and relationship. There is no fear in His love because His love casts out all of our fears. When you are with Him, time does not matter, tragedy doesn't hurt, and pain dissipates. I don't mind being vulnerable to Him because I know He won't hurt me; He won't harm me. I may have been wounded, but not by Him! They may criticize me, but He speaks words of love into my ears as I rest in His presence. A thousand shall fall at my side and ten thousand at my right hand, but they will not come anywhere near me. I am in the shelter of the Almighty!

Intimacy means that I have trust in the person that I am in relationship with. I trust them enough to give them complete access to my whole being. I don't cover or hide from them when I am in the place of intimacy. As a matter of fact, I am drawn to be exposed and vulnerable to them. I want them to know that I trust them with ME! I want them to understand that I am placing who I am into their hands. And I know that the safest place in the whole wide world is in the Master's Hands.

Know this, people of God: You never lose when you are intimate with Him; you only gain. As you set yourself to be in a deep and intimate relationship with Him; when you come to Him, He will not cast you aside! He will take you up into His secret pavilion, constructed personally for YOU! He longs to be close to you. He longs for you to be fully surrendered to Him. Intimacy cries out, "Take me as I am and be to me everything I need!" The Lord does not disappoint. He will be all that you need and more. If you need that friend, He will be that to you. If you need comfort, the Holy Ghost will comfort you. If you need healing, the healing virtue from Calvary will flow in your direction. He will not disappoint you. You will be fully satisfied in His presence.

Chapter 7

Obedience

Doing it God's way is what obedience means to me. Proverbs 16:25 reads, *"There is a way that seemeth right unto a man, but the end thereof are the ways of death."* To worship God His way, we must serve, worship and work in the Kingdom. Case in point, Aaron had two sons sanctified to be priests in the house of the Lord. Their names were Nadab and Abihu. In Leviticus 10, they thought their way of offering incense in the tabernacle was okay, but they paid with their lives for their irreverence, presumption and disobedience.

Leviticus 10: 1-3: And Nadab and Abihu, the sons of Aaron, took either of them his censer and put fire therein, and put incense thereon, and offered strange fire before the LORD, which he commanded them not. And there went out fire from the LORD, and devoured them, and they died before the LORD. Then Moses said unto Aaron, This is it that the LORD spake, saying, I will be sanctified in them that come nigh me, and before all the people I will be glorified. And Aaron held his peace.

In the book of Leviticus, God gave details as to how He was to be worshipped. He specified the types of offerings; He gave specific details about what was to be offered, and He made it clear who it was that could present the offerings. He repeatedly made it plain to His leaders and His people that He was and is a holy God. He demands holiness of us on a daily basis. He said, *"Be holy as I am holy" (See Leviticus 11:44).* In the scriptures, God is repeatedly trying to teach an unholy people how to approach a holy God. I'm assuming that in the minds of Aaron's sons, the details of worshipping God His way didn't matter that much. Why didn't it matter? They were priests, and they knew how to go before God. They assumed it was okay to bring some common fire to offer in the house of God. For them, it had to be okay; God wouldn't mind. After all, they were HIS priests. The bible says that when they were making their offering before the Lord, they knew it was wrong; nevertheless, they did it anyway. Many people go before a HOLY God any old kind of way and expect it to be alright with Him. As a matter of fact, they know that it's wrong, but because they feel that they have a special relationship with God, they figure they are going to do it anyway. The bible said that Aaron's sons offered before God what He commanded them not to. As soon as they did this, there went out a fire from the Lord Himself and devoured them, and they died before the Lord. Bringing strange fire into the house of the Lord was an act of irreverence. They had NO respect for the things of God. Irreverence is defined as:

1. The quality of being irreverent; lack of reverence or respect.
2. An irreverent act or statement.
3. The condition of not being reverenced, venerated, respected, etc.

Reverence:

1. A feeling or attitude of deep respect tinged with awe; veneration.
2. The outward manifestation of this feeling: to pay reverence.
3. A gesture indicative of deep respect; an obeisance, bow, or curtsy.

(Reference: Dictionary.Reference.com)

If the young men of God gave Him the much needed and deserving respect that He was due; if they showed Him the awe (overwhelming feeling of reverence, admiration and fear) that He was requiring them, they would not have committed such an act. Their act was an act if irreverence, not respecting His requirements. They took it upon themselves to offer whatever seemed right to them at the time. They took for granted their positions in the ministry. They probably believed that this little misstep would be passed over by the Lord. The bottom line is: they disobeyed God and thought they would get off easy. That just doesn't happen with the things of God.

This reminds me of Cain and Abel. They were both taught by their parents the proper way to make an offering before God. Abel brought his best; Cain brought whatever he could find before the Lord. The bible says that God had respect for Abel's offering, but not

Cain's. Abel gave God what He wanted. He respected God's wants and His desires. Cain was upset because his offering wasn't accepted; nevertheless, God demonstrated His approval of Abel's offering. In so many words, God was saying to Cain that if he did what God asked of Him, he would receive God's approval. God would go on to say that if we do it our own way, sin is lying at our doors, and we must master it before it masters us. I Samuel 22:15 says *"And Samuel said, hath the Lord great delight in burnt offerings and sacrifices as in obeying the voice of the Lord? Behold to obey is better than sacrifice and to hearken than the fat of rams."* It's not necessarily the offering that He is seeking, but the obedience to the Lord of the offering.

Because Nadab and Abihu did not obey Him, God judged them on the spot, and they died before the Lord. Back in the days of the law, obedience preserved the life of the people. As the people obeyed the Word of the Lord, they reaped the benefits. Warning comes before destruction. God gives us the right, proper and acceptable way of approaching Him, because God really wants to have fellowship with us. He wants us in His presence; He takes delight in His children spending time with Him, just like any father delights in his children.

Moses reproved Aaron and reminded him of what the Lord said. God said that He would be sanctified (set apart, made holy, not made common but shown, demonstrated by them to be separate) by those that come near to Him. God will be reverenced by those who approach Him, and if you are representing Him before all the people, you will glorify (exalt, praise, worship, extol, cause to seem more splendid) Him. In other words, He will be treated as God; holy, sanctified, separated, when you approach Him as your God, and He will be represented as your God. He is worthy of worship, honor, praise and adoration when we go before the people in His name. As His representatives and ambassadors, we represent Him; re-present Him. What we do is show God to the people of God. That is why we must be careful how we re-present Him in the earth. Are we giving the world the right picture of our God? If we follow His instructions, we demonstrate the picture that is needed to be shown to the world.

Chapter 8

Commitment

The FreeDictionary.com defines commitment as:

The act or an instance of committing, especially:

a. The act of referring a legislative bill to committee.

b. Official consignment, as to a prison or mental health facility.

c. A court order authorizing consignment to a prison

Commitment to the Lord is extremely important if we seek to really please the One we say that we want to please. Commitment is a requirement if we desire to be His followers. It is a requirement that we worship Him in Spirit and in truth. The Lord deserves and demands our total commitment to Him and Him alone. In Exodus 20: 1–6, the Lord instructs us this way:

"And God spake all these words, saying, I am the LORD thy God, which have brought thee out of the land of Egypt, out of the house of bondage. Thou shalt have no other gods before me. Thou shalt not make unto thee any graven image, or any likeness of anything that is in heaven above, or that is in the earth beneath, or that is in the water under the earth: Thou shalt not bow down thyself to them, nor serve them: for I the LORD thy God am a jealous God, visiting the iniquity of the fathers upon the children unto the third and fourth generation of them that hate me; And shewing mercy unto thousands of them that love me, and keep my commandments."

In this text, the Lord reminds us that He is the One that saved and delivered the children of Israel out of bondage, and He commands and demands our complete commitment to Him. He is the One who, according to John 3:16 "*so loved the world that He gave His only begotten son, that whosoever believes in Him should not perish …*" He has loved and delivered us in a way that no one else could or would. Why not commit to Him? This is the One who ransomed us from prison and bought us off of the slave block of sin. We owe Him our spiritual lives. This is the One who basically says, "I know you have made a mess of yourself, a mess of your life and a mess of your walk; yet knowing all of this, I love you, and I want you as My very own prized possession. I want to show you off to the world as My own beautiful child." He does not force it on us, though; He gives us an invitation. The choice is ours.

The FreeDictionary.com defines pledge as:

1. a formal or solemn promise or agreement, esp to do or refrain from doing something
2. collateral for the payment of a debt or the performance of an obligation the condition of being collateral (esp in the phrase in pledge)
3. a sign, token, or indication the gift is a pledge of their sincerity
4. an assurance of support or goodwill, conveyed by drinking to a person, cause, etc.; toast we drank a pledge to their success
5. a person who binds himself, as by becoming bail or surety for another

Who would not pledge or commit his life to serving the One who paid his debt in full for sin? I think about all I have done in the form of sin; how I lied, how I cheated. I said some things and done some things that I knew were wrong, but God forgave me, loved me, and saved me again and again from myself and from situations. Thinking about all of what I've done and how He still loves me, I go into such a place of deep love, adoration and worship! I have to give Him what is due Him; I give Him all of me. I lift my hands to tell Him "thank you." I walk the floors and thank Him. I lie on the floor, roll on the floor, dance on the floor in worship for my redemption and my Redeemer. I commit myself, pledge myself, and bind myself to the exclusive worship of Him and Him alone!

My commitment means I restrict myself from running after some other thing to give my worship to. I pledge, or make a formal commitment, to be faithful and true to Him. I know that He has my best interest at heart when He makes a decision. My commitment makes me hand over myself for safe keeping into the hands of the true and living God. It means that I place my full trust in who He is and what He is doing in my life. I pledge my life to Him; I obligate myself to serve Him because He paid my debt in full. In return for His love, I freely give Him a life of service and servanthood! As I walk in trust towards Him, He has already demonstrated He is the Lover of my soul. He did this by giving His best to me and for me. So in return, I give Him my hand, my heart and my life as I commit myself to Him. As I walk in this commitment, His strong arm and mighty hand shelters and protects me. I am secure in His love. I know He loves me, and He knows I love Him. Our love reminds me of the Song of Solomon when it says:

Song of Solomon 1:2-4-*"Let him kiss me with the kisses of his mouth: for thy love is better*

than wine. Because of the savior of thy good ointments thy name is as ointment poured forth, therefore do the virgins love thee. Draw me, we will run after thee: the king hath brought me into his chambers: we will be glad and rejoice in thee, we will remember thy love more than wine: the upright love thee."
Song of Solomon 2:2–4- *"As the lily among thorns, so is my love among the daughters. As the apple tree among the trees of the wood, so is my beloved among the sons. I sat down under his shadow with great delight, and his fruit was sweet to my taste. He brought me to the banqueting house, and his banner over me was love."*

I restrict myself from giving my spiritual love, my devoted worship to anyone other than the One who is loading me down with benefits on a daily basis *(See Psalm 68:19)*. I give myself freely to the One who makes my feet like hind's feet and causes me to set upon my high places (*See Psalm 18:33*). How can I not love on the One who didn't let my enemies get the best of me, but set my feet in a large, prosperous room (*See Psalm 31:8*)? I am secure with His love. His banner over me and His covering for me is love, and I am committed to His love. At the same time, He has committed Himself to loving me forever. He said, *"Lo I am with you always even unto the end of the world" (Matthew28:20).* It is powerful knowing that, after death, we will not part from one another. Praise God that HE WILL ALWAYS BE WITH ME, AND I WILL ALWAYS BE WITH HIM.

All the same, He is committed to being WITH me. He will be with me when things are good and when things are not so good. He sends rain in my direction when I'm dry, and He waters those hidden places that I sometimes try to cover. He gives heat in cold seasons; that is when folks are giving me the cold shoulder. He meets me early in the morning with new mercies to carry me through the day. He is my daily sustainer; giving me bread to nourish my body, soul and mind! He opens up the windows of heaven and pours me out a blessing that I don't have room enough to receive. He is committed to taking care of us, people of God!

He is the One who comforts me when times get rough. Sometimes, it's His loving presence that embraces me, and sometimes, He sends a saint along to hug me too! When I'm lost and hurting in the middle of the night, I can feel Him camped at my bedside encouraging me to hold on because morning is coming. When I cry, He sees my tears and catches every one of them in a bottle. He lets me rest in meadows of grass, and He leads me beside the quiet stream (*See Psalm 23*). I love the line in the song *Safe In His Arms*, that reads, *"He restores my failing health, and He helps me to do what honors Him the most. That's why I'm safe I His arms."* He loves on me so hard that He holds the world together by the power of His Word! Everything in my life is held together by His Word!

When I compare what He's done and what He continues to do in my life with what I do and give to Him, there is no comparison. The old folks used to say, "You can't beat God giving, no matter how hard you try." Why is that? Because the more you give, the more He gives to you! He beats you every time. Because the earth is the Lord's and the fullness thereof: the world and they that dwell therein (*See Psalm 24:1*). Whatever I give Him already belongs to Him, even myself!

My commitment is a choice and a

decision to remain true to Him. I set myself to worship and praise Him exclusively for who He is and what He continues to do in my life. I give myself to Him daily in prayer so that He can fill me with more and more of Himself. He fills me so I can look more like Him and live more like Him. I want to represent Him in this world. I live to represent Him in this world. My commitment to Him is required if I want to truly worship Him!

Part III

Looking Forward In Worship

Chapter 9

An Ear To Hear- New Songs/New Ways

God is releasing new songs in the atmosphere for worship. Jesus says *"But the hour cometh and now is when the true worshipper shall worship the Father in spirit and in truth: for the Father seeketh such to worship Him. God is a Spirit: and they that worship Him must worship Him in spirit and in truth" (John 4:23-24).* It is time to worship the Father as He desires it. He is seeking those who will reach out to Him and worship Him from within their spirit. Those who go after Him in such a manner will receive keys that will unlock realms and dimensions in the spirit.

They will receive new songs, new weapons and new methods to take back the things that have been pilfered from the people of God; this will be part of the reward!

The new songs that will be released will free those who hear them. The songs will come straight out of the realms of the Spirit. The songs will be songs of healing and deliverance. They will be songs of war and songs that bring peace. He will release songs to the true worshippers that will push us higher into new dimensions, causing us to battle the enemy with renewed strength. The new songs will release strategies to engage the enemy and defeat him to anyone who hears them. The songs, people of God, will be the children's bread! God said, "Seek me in those new realms, and it will yield powerful fruit to increase My Kingdom on earth."

One of the callings that He has gifted
me with is to hear songs in the Spirit. I can
hear the heart cry of heaven and sing it into the
ears of those who are on earth. I can also hear
the hearts of God's people, and He will give me
a song of healing and deliverance for them.
Oftentimes, it catapults the listener into a new
place in Him. I am so grateful to God! We must
have an ear to hear what the Spirit is saying to
the church, and we must have ears to hear
what the Spirit is singing to the church as well.
It is time we put on our spiritual listening
devices; they will cause us to pick up those
frequencies that emanate from heaven. Those
frequencies are only discernible in levels and
dimensions of corporate and even private
worship times. We must posture ourselves
spiritually to hear heavenly songs. We can no
longer come to church with the "church as
usual" mindset. We must earnestly seek and
desire for a fresh word and a fresh move of His

Holy Spirit. We must invite Him in to move radically and supernaturally in our midst. We have to push in worship for the Spirit of God to manifest Himself. When I say that we have to push in worship for manifestation, I mean that we cannot be satisfied with the ordinary; we must push past the old to get to the new. Sometimes, we have to sing past our ordinary songs and ask the Holy Ghost to sing through us. Life-changing experiences are what we should crave in every worship experience. Lord knows we need so much more in the atmosphere to move the enemy out of the lives of the people of God so that the Spirit of God is drawn closer to us. We need fresh manna for the people of God in praise and worship to help renew mindsets. Let us thank Him in advance for the new songs.

People of God, we can't just come to service and sit down to be entertained. We must come with our hands lifted up in worship, our eyes closed, our mouth open to give thanks to Him and our hearts open to receive from Him. We need to come with our ears open so that we will be in tune with what The Lord wants to say to His people. Make your commitment to be an active participant in this spiritual process. Give yourself to Him while in the midst of the congregation and watch what happens to you and those around you.

But please don't just be satisfied with it happening in your local assembly; why not shoot for the same experience at home? Set aside time at home where you wait in His presence. Mark a place that you will meet with Him every day. This is not something new; it's something we just don't do as much as we should. The truth is: what you do at home shows up when you get to the house of God. If you do nothing during the week, you will have nothing to offer God and His people. We must understand that since we want more in our worship experiences, it will definitely cost us more. I don't want entertainment when it comes to worship, what I want is my Father. Jesus was so powerful on earth because He spent so much time with His Father. That is what we need to do right now to receive a fresh move from our Father in heaven.

There is a freshness that is coming to the body of Christ. This freshness is beginning to fall because the children of God desires it, and these same children are hungering and thirsting after it. There is a heart cry for more of the Father, more of His Spirit and more of His manifest presence. There is a desire to be positioned for personal change. This is the seeking that the Father has been longing for. Just like any Father, God wants to give His children good gifts. Not just gifts that show off

the latest rifts and runs in singing, but gifts that
shift atmospheres and change lives. The
Father wants to release these gifts to His
children, but it will happen in our time. As we
prepare for the arrival of our soon coming King,
He is trying to get His bride cleansed and
ready. This freshness will aid us, making us
ready to meet Him. This freshness that is
beginning to fall is moving us to draw near to
Him.

There has been a stirring in our hearts
to draw near to Him. James 4:8 says, *"Draw
nigh to God and He will draw nigh to you.
Cleanse your hands, ye sinners; and purify
your hearts, ye double minded."* James 4:10
goes on to say, *"Humble yourselves under the
mighty hand of God and He will lift you up."*
There is a drive brewing in the people of God
to get closer to God and His ways. It is this
yearning after clean hands and a pure heart

(*See Psalm 24*) that is driving the people of God into a powerful worship encounter with their God. Understand that the Spirit of the Lord is drawing us closer to Him. What's happening is that we feel this pull or tug on our own spirits. We are saying to God, "I feel you drawing me, and I want to come, but I have so much in the way." The Word tells us to cleanse ourselves of our busyness and draw near to Him. Purify your hearts from those things that are dividing you from Him. Wash that heart clean with the Word and with His presence. God says, "I want to come closer to you! You need Me to come closer to you for this end-time freshness and newness to take hold in you."

As we are cleansed and He draws near to us, our minds are settled in the right place to receive the newness and freshness that He wants to give to us. Romans 12:2 says, *"And*

*be not conformed to the world but be ye
transformed by the renewing of your mind..."*
Ephesians 4:23 says that we should *"be
renewed in the spirit of our minds."* It's sad to
say, but sometimes when you look at the
church, you see more of the world than
representations of Him. The fighting, lying,
sexing that we are used to in the world has
infiltrated the church. Week after week, some
preacher, pastor or leader is stepping down
because of some sexual sin, be it adultery,
homosexuality, or any other form of sexual
immorality. Members are finding themselves in
more compromising situations. Instead of our
hands being clean, they are dirty from what we
are doing, and our minds are unclean from the
things we have been watching and meditating
on. The bible tells us that as a man thinks in his
heart, so is he. Whatever we meditate on is
what we become. If we meditate on things
instead of the Source of everything, we miss

the hand of God, and these impure things will cause our garments to be dirty. Our garments are spotted and soiled from the cares of this world. The bride, as we know her, is dirty and needs a deep cleansing. The Father is sending His Spirit in these last hours to clean up His bride, but the biggest challenge for us is in our minds. We have filled it with everything but what we need. That is why we must be renewed in our minds. Our minds need to be renewed from the trash and filth of the world and changed into the righteousness and holiness that is God. The cleansing process will not only assist us in drawing near to Him, but as we get closer to Him, He speaks a renewing into our inward man and our mindset. This newness aids in flushing the old ways out and makes room for the new information, strategies and songs that He wants to release to us for His body. A renewed mind allows God to shift us to where we should be or should have been.

A renewed mind shifts us away from the ways of the world to the mind of Christ!

Thirdly, as our minds are cleansed and renewed, it brings us into our rightful attitude, which is humility. The bible tells us that we must humble ourselves. In most cases, we pray and ask God to humble us. I remember singing, "Humble me, humble me, oh Lord!" I wanted God to come down and do the work of humbling me. The thought of what God would do to humble me is very sobering. That is why He says to us, "You do it! Humble yourself under My mighty hand. Put some effort into bringing down your own pride. Kill that attitude that says you are better than everyone or everything." We must realize that it is by the grace of God that we are who we are, and that we have what we have. We need to thank Him every day. Know that it is of the Lord's mercy that we are not consumed, because His compassions fail not; they are new every morning *(See Lamentations 3:22)*. If we would have gotten what we deserved, we would be done; but thank the Lord that His compassion fails not! If I examined myself in the light of His holiness, I would be just like Isaiah; I would be undone. Yet in the light of all of my spiritual poverty, the King still wants to use me for His glory. This is an honor! I am humbled at the thought that the King wants to use me. He wants to use crazy, mixed up, broken down me to serve His people. But not just me; He wants to use you too! His love is so amazing!

As we take our proper attitudes and positions of humility, He is able to lift us up into those new, fresh places. He allows the rain of that freshness to fall on us all the more. He can only trust those who have trusted Him enough to let Him transform them with new information. He essentially says, "You trusted Me with this,

so I am going to give you that." What is "that"?
"That" is new places, new doors, new
opportunities and strategies. New songs of
worship emerge as He downloads new
information into us. People of God, it is on the
way! As He lifts us up, He brings us to higher
places in the heavenlies, where we hear and
see things we have never heard or seen
before. When Paul was discussing his
experiences with the people of God, he said he
was taken up to a place and saw things that he
had no words for. I would venture to say that
since this is information that the Lord wants His
people to receive, we will be able to translate it
into some things that are useful to the Body of
Christ. I am pressing into Him for songs that
have never been sung on this side of glory. I
am seeking after experiences that will rival the
Smith Wigglesworth days. I am searching for
times in His presence that will so transform me
and those around me that people will come in

off the streets desiring what we have and what we are experiencing.

Do you not know that one right song that is sung in due season can destroy yokes in a person's life that have been sitting there for years? One right word spoken in time can tear down years of pain, sorrow and suffering. I want that word or that song in my mouth that is given to me by my Father in heaven. I want to be the vessel that delivers a nation. If God can use anyone, I want Him to use me. Don't you want to be a part of this end time army?

Chapter 10

End Time Army Tools

In the previous chapter, we talked about new moves into His presence that will bring about freshness for the true worshippers. We talked about new songs that will be released from heaven. We will spend this final chapter on the new strategies in warfare that He will be releasing to us in the realms of the Spirit as we press further into His presence. God is not just releasing new songs, but He is also releasing new strategies of spiritual warfare. But also note that in terms of warfare, there is nothing new under the sun. What He is releasing is the same as what He released before, yet somehow different! It may sound contradictory, but it's not.

Let's look first at some of God's unusual styles of battle plans that brought about victory for the people of God. First of all, God had given Joshua a very unusual battle plan to take Jericho. Now, Jericho was a fenced in city and almost impossible to take. Joshua 6 reads: *"Now Jericho was straitly shut up because of the children of Israel: none went out, and none came in. And the LORD said unto Joshua, See, I have given into thine hand Jericho, and the king thereof, and the mighty men of valour. And ye shall compass the city, all ye men of war, and go round about the city once . Thus shalt thou do six days. And seven priests shall bear before the ark seven trumpets of rams' horns: and the seventh day ye shall compass the city seven times, and the priests shall blow with the trumpets. And it shall come to pass, that when they make a long blast with the ram's horn, and when ye hear the sound of the trumpet, all the people shall shout with a great shout; and the wall of the city shall fall down flat, and the people shall ascend up every man straight before him. And Joshua the son of Nun called the priests, and said unto them, Take up the ark of the covenant, and let seven priests bear seven trumpets of rams' horns before the ark of the LORD. And he said unto the people, Pass on , and compass the city, and let him that is armed pass on before the ark of the LORD. And it came to pass, when Joshua had spoken unto the people, that the seven priests bearing the seven trumpets of rams' horns passed on before the LORD, and blew with the trumpets: and the ark of the covenant of the LORD followed them. And the armed men went before the priests that blew with the trumpets, and the rereward came after the ark, the priests going on , and blowing with the trumpets. And Joshua had commanded the*

*people, saying , Ye shall not shout , nor make
any noise with your voice, neither shall any
word proceed out of your mouth, until the day I
bid you shout ; then shall ye shout."*

Now look at it this way: The Lord was
basically saying, "I've given you this city, but
you have to take it MY way. I want you to
parade around the city like you already have
the victory, but don't say anything or let anyone
know it yet. You must obey Me to the letter if
you want to walk away with the victory. And
make sure you tell all the people of God not to
speak so they don't blow it for you and
everyone else." As stated in the previous
chapter, obedience is the key in any operation
for the King. If you're not going to do it His way,
prepare to lose. What causes us to win in any
battle is complete obedience. What happens
with us sometimes is we get really good ideas
that we want to attach to what He says. It may

be a good idea, but it becomes disobedience when we add to or take away from what He said. The Lord says walk around the city in worship, and you will win this battle. Let there not be a sound of murmuring, complaining, fear or worry. Just worship the King in all His holiness. Continue to do it until He says different. There are battles before us that we have to win, and we can only win them the way He says. Worship is such a powerful tool that it shifts your attention from the problem to the Problem-solver. Worship takes your eyes off of self and places them on to the One that created you. Worship fixes us in such a way that it empowers us to go forward and take an impossible situation. Most armies could not take Jericho because it was a fortified city; nevertheless, ask yourself: What is a wall to a God who creates walls and takes them down? Walls are nothing to the obedient servant of God either. You can worship your way around them, through them, under them and over them. Obedience is powerful!

The key to winning the war in Jericho was obedience. That is an unusual weapon. We consider ourselves very intelligent and capable of making rational choices and decisions, but He knows the WAY that He wants to take us. His way will always prosper us and give us His expected end. His expected way will always bless us. His way is connected to our future success. It is an end-time tool in our arsenal.

Another tool in our arsenal is anointed worship that proclaims the truth of God. In the book of Kings, Joshua was facing an army that was much greater that his. He sought the Lord and got direction.

Another tool in our powerful tool box is

breakthrough prayer, or better yet, a powerful prayer life. In the Garden of Gethsemane, Jesus was about to face the enemy head on. Before He arrived in Jerusalem, it was His custom to spend time with His Father to get wisdom, guidance instruction and strength. You see, Jesus did not do anything without first consulting the Father. If you want to win some battles, consult the Father about the challenge before you enter the challenge. Get the wisdom of the Father to see if it is a battle you should go into. Think about David's plight. David had just lost everything. His family and all he possessed was gone. He had an army that wanted to stone him; nevertheless, David worshipped God in the midst of his situation.

What does the worshipper do? He consults the Father. He asks the Lord, "Should I pursue them; should I go after them? Lord, You run this thing. I know I want to do my own thing in this situation, but what would You advise me to do? You know the end of this matter from the beginning; what should I do?" This puts the onus on Him to take us over, around or through the situation. With His directions, we will always win!

Let's go back to the garden. Jesus was about to face the cross. He wanted to do the will of God, but it looked very difficult in that hour. Jesus saw the pain, agony and struggle that was in the whole crucifixion scene. He saw His disciples leaving Him. He saw the betrayer coming. It is hard when all hell is literally coming against you. What can a believer do? *"Seek Him where He may be found. Call upon Him while He is near"* (Isaiah 55:6).

Finally our last tool in the arsenal is learning how to wait. *"In your patience possess ye your souls"* (Luke 21:19).

Timing is everything when it concerns the things of God. How many times did Jesus say, "It is not yet my time?" You must move in the timing of God. Sometimes, you just have to wait! *"But they that wait upon the LORD shall renew their strength; they shall mount up with wings as eagles; they shall run, and not be weary; and they shall walk, and not faint"* *(Isaiah 40:31).* Wait on the Lord and be of good strength, and He will strengthen thine heart.